If you don't believe this airline pilot is a woman, you'd better look again.

Butcher, Baker, Cabinetmaker
Photographs of Women at Work

Photography by Abigail Heyman   **Text by Wendy Saul**

Thomas Y. Crowell   New York

Photographs copyright © 1978 by Abigail Heyman
Text copyright © 1978 by E. Wendy Saul

Kromeltone Reproductions & Printing
By Pearl Pressman-Liberty, Philadelphia, Pa.

Library of Congress Cataloging in Publication Data

Heyman, Abigail.
    Butcher, baker, cabinetmaker.
    SUMMARY: Photographs and text introduce women
employed in jobs traditionally reserved for men.
    1. Women—Employment—Pictorial works—Juvenile
literature. [1. Women—Employment—Pictorial works]
1. Saul, Wendy   II. Title.
HD6053.H48   331.4'022'2   77-27668
ISBN 0-690-03899-2   0-690-03900-X lib. bdg.

First Edition

Designed by Arnold Skolnick

This is a book about women who work.

Can you think of work you have seen women do?

Here is an astronaut who works
with a team of scientists
to discover new facts
about outer space.

This artist chooses to work alone,

painting on canvas

what she sees.

This letter carrier enjoys working outside,

seeing the neighborhood and meeting people

who are waiting for their mail.

As an architect this woman likes to design houses

that will make life comfortable and interesting

for the people who move into them.

There are many jobs that women can do and many reasons why they work.

Most women work because they need the money they earn.

This lawyer uses her money to buy groceries for herself and her family.

Some women do not get paid for the work they do,

but they work very hard anyway, like this parent

who cares for her child...

or this athlete, who practices each day.

Sometimes the name of the job tells us
whether a worker is a man or a woman.
The fire department hires "firemen" and
"firewomen," but now calls them both "fire fighters"
since both do the same work.

Every worker must learn how to do her job.

These women—a farmer and a store owner—

learned what they need to know

by working with family, friends, and neighbors.

Sometimes, like all workers,

they just figure out things for themselves.

This coal miner and this radio reporter

were taught their jobs by the people they work for,

although they could have learned many of the same kinds of skills

by going to special training schools.

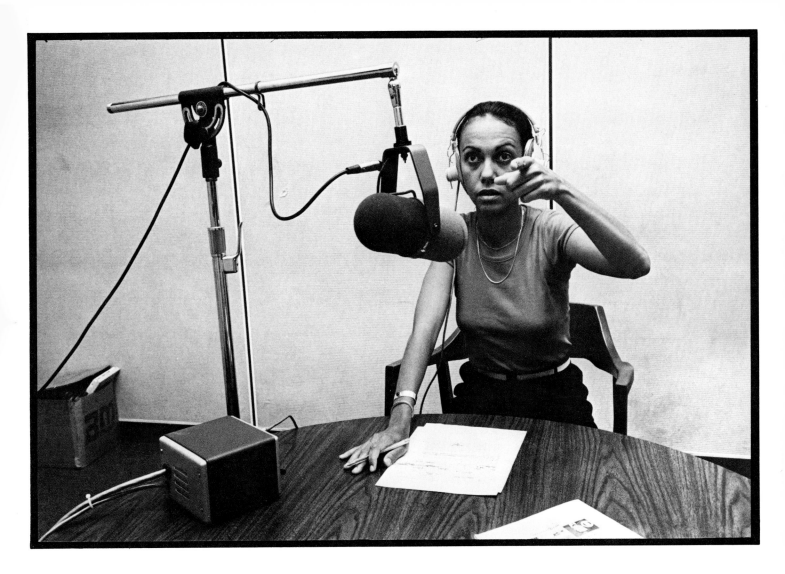

Other workers, like this biologist who studies tiny fruitflies

and this veterinarian who doctors pets,

have gone to school for many, many years

to learn about the work they do.

What must these women know to do their jobs well?

This woman is a carpenter.

She builds things made of wood.

Can you name some of the tools she uses?

Other women use other tools in their work—a gas pump...

or costumes and makeup.

Here is a woman who works

as a zoo keeper.

She takes care of snakes,

lizards, crocodiles, and turtles.

She feeds them,

and cleans their cages

and sees that they

are feeling fine.

If the walls are peeling, or dirty, or a color you dislike...

this woman can paint the place.

Can you guess what this woman does?

Look at the building where she works.

She might be a museum director,

or a school principal,

or a fashion model...

but she's not.

In fact she is a state senator, and she works in the state capital.

She helps to make laws for the people of New Jersey.

She got her job because people in her state voted for her.

This woman drives a milk truck from dairy farms to a bottling plant.

Before she puts the milk in her truck...

she takes samples for her company.

Later the samples are tested

to make sure the milk is

clean and creamy enough for you.

This orchestra conductor decides how the music should be played.

She uses her hands and a baton to give directions to the musicians.

They must watch her very carefully.

Sometimes this girl thinks about becoming a musician.

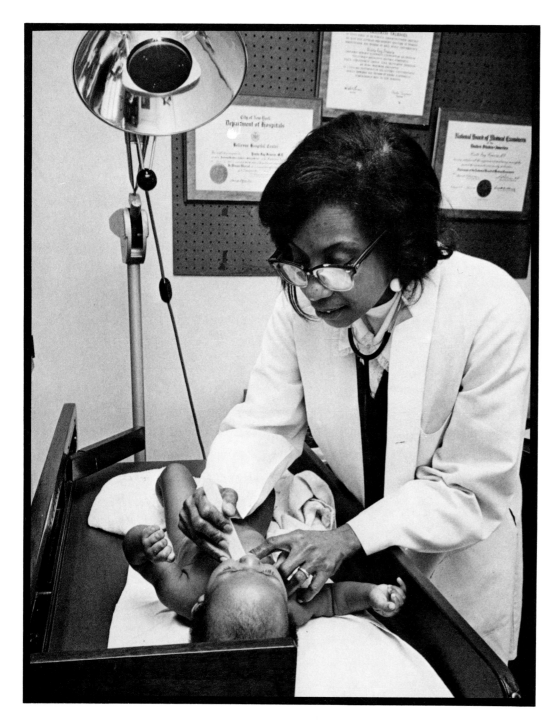

Have you thought about
the work you want to do
when you are older?

What work do you do now?

1   Pilot: Cheryl Ritchie, Piedmont Airlines

2   Astronaut: Judith A. Resnik, PhD, National Aeronautics and Space Administration

3   Artist: Mary Petruska

5   Architect: Suzanne H. Crowhurst Lennard, PhD

We thank these women, and the people they work with, for sharing their work lives with us:

6, 7   Lawyer: Rachael Adams, JD, VISTA

4   Letter carrier: Janet Williamson, United States Postal Service

9   Athlete: Mary Concordia, Rutgers University

8   Parent: Ginger Hupp with daughter Laura Hupp

10, 11   Fire fighter: Judy Livers,
Arlington, Virginia, Fire Department

12   Farmer:
Bunny Scot

13   Store owner: Libby
Sangster, Antiques-on-the-
Hill, Washington, D.C.

14   Coal miner: Sarah Dockins and friends, Mead
Coal Company, Alabama

15   Radio reporter: Kate Williams, Station KSJN,
Minneapolis Public Radio

17   Veterinarian:
Marguerite B. Gulick, VMD

16   Biologist:
Eileen Gersh, PhD,
University of
Pennsylvania

18   Taxi driver: Joanie Fiore

19 Butcher: Carolyn Canevari, Canevari Meat Market, New York City

20, 21 Carpenter: Lorna McNeur

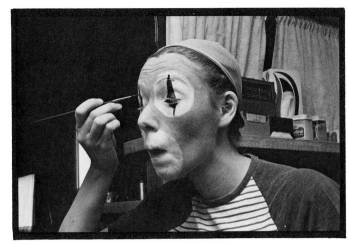

23 Clown: Coco Leigh, Famous Hunt's Circus

22 Airport linesperson: Aspen, Colorado, Airport

24, 25 Zoo keeper: Sarah Cumins, Philadelphia Zoo

26, 27 House painter: Carol Goebel, Dutch Girl Painters, New York City

28–31 State senator: Alene Ammond, New Jersey State Senate

32, 33 Milk-truck driver: Pat Waite, Foremost Food Company, California

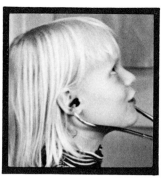

34   Orchestra conductor: Judith Somogi, with the Naumburg Symphony Orchestra

35   Child with drums: Eve Lippman

36   Doctor: Yvette Francis, MD

37   Child with stethoscope: Natasha Zweig with her mother, Gitte Zweig

Child with horse (right): Sara Katz

38   Child drawing: Keyra Figueroa
Children running: Natasha Schull and Beth Brown
Child reading: Larissa Heyman

39   Children with skateboard: Christie Smit and Josh Eric Goldman
Children in school: Keyra Figueroa, and Elsa Mercedes de Peña

I am Abigail Heyman.

As a photographer, I use a camera to make pictures like those you've seen in museums, on television, in magazines, or in books like this one. As a parent, I take care of one-year-old Lazar Heyman-Bloch, as does his father. I photographed the women in this book with the hope that Lazar and all children will enjoy the satisfactions, and the fun, of working hard.

I am Wendy Saul.

I have worked as a farmer, a factory worker, a student, a teacher, a professor, a feminist organizer, and a writer. Now I spend most of my work time thinking, reading, writing, and teaching about old and new children's books. I wrote the text for this book because I like talking to children about a world in which both girls and boys have real choices about who and what they want to be.